William Blake

by MARTIN BUTLIN

TATE GALLERY Published by Order of the Trustees 1975

BARRON'S
WOODBURY, NEW YORK

ISBN 0 900874 37 6
Copyright © 1966 Tate Gallery   2nd impression 1968   3rd impression 1972   4th impression 1975
Published by the Tate Gallery Publications Department, Millbank, London, SW1P 4RG
Printed in Great Britain by Balding + Mansell, London and Wisbech

LIST OF PLATES

16 *The Blasphemer. c.* 1800
Pen and watercolour, $15 \times 13\frac{3}{8}$ in.
(5195)

17 *Satan in his Original Glory. c.* 1800–5
Pen and watercolour, $16\frac{7}{8} \times 13\frac{3}{8}$ in.
(5892)

18 *The Four and Twenty Elders. c.* 1805
Pencil and watercolour,
$13\frac{15}{16} \times 11\frac{1}{2}$ in. (5897)

19 *Sketch for The Four and Twenty
Elders. c.* 1805
Pencil, $19 \times 15\frac{1}{8}$ in. (3694 i recto)

20 *The Spiritual Form of Pitt guiding
Behemoth.* 1805
Tempera on canvas, $29\frac{1}{8} \times 24\frac{3}{4}$ in.
(1110)

21 *The Spiritual Form of Nelson
guiding Leviathan. c.* 1805–9
Tempera on canvas, $30 \times 24\frac{5}{8}$ in.
(3006)

22 *The Body of Abel found by Adam
and Eve. c.* 1826
Tempera on panel, $12\frac{3}{4} \times 17$ in.
(5888)

23 *Satan smiting Job with Sore Boils.
c.* 1826
Tempera on panel, $12\frac{7}{8} \times 17$ in.
(3340)

24 *The Man who built the Pyramids*
(? copy by John Linnell).
1819 ?
Pencil, $11\frac{7}{8} \times 8\frac{1}{2}$ in. (5185)

25 *The Ghost of a Flea. c.* 1819
Tempera on panel, $8\frac{7}{16} \times 6\frac{3}{8}$ in.
(5889)

26 *The Simoniac Pope.* 1824–7
Pen and watercolour, $20\frac{3}{4} \times 14\frac{1}{2}$ in.
(3357)

27 *The Inscription over the Gate of Hell.*
1824–7
Pen and watercolour, $20\frac{5}{8} \times 14\frac{1}{2}$ in.
(3352)

28 *Dante and Virgil penetrating the
Forest.* 1824–7
Pencil, pen and watercolour,
$14\frac{1}{2} \times 20\frac{5}{8}$ in. (3351)

29 *The Pit of Disease: the Falsifiers.*
1824–7
Pen and watercolour, $14\frac{5}{8} \times 20\frac{5}{8}$ in.
(3362)

30 *Dante and Virgil approaching the
Angel who guards the Entrance of
Purgatory.* 1824–7
Pencil, pen and watercolour,
$20\frac{5}{8} \times 14\frac{5}{8}$ in. (3367)

31 *Beatrice addressing Dante from the
Car.* 1824–7
Pen and watercolour, $14\frac{5}{8} \times 20\frac{3}{4}$ in.
(3369)

32 *Dante in the Empyrean, drinking at
the River of Light.* 1824–7
Pencil and watercolour, $20\frac{5}{8} \times 14\frac{5}{8}$ in.
(3370)

WILLIAM BLAKE 1757–1827

The Blake collection at the Tate Gallery is the most representative selection of his work readily available to the public. It comprises all phases of his career and every kind of subject. It does not however include any of his illuminated books. More important, it must be remembered that Blake's work in the visual arts was only half his achievement, his poetry being one of the glories of English literature.

There is a particularly close relationship between Blake's writings and his designs. Not that the latter are merely illustrations to his writings; rather, both writings and designs were regarded by Blake as the expression of a single Poetic or Prophetic Genius. Only through this Genius could eternal truths be apprehended and this alone was the justification of art.

Blake's art was based on a fully thought out philosophy, but during his life this underwent certain changes. In particular the revolutionary ideas of his early years, when he was associated with such political radicals as Joseph Johnson, Thomas Paine, Joseph Priestley, Mary Woolstonecraft and William Godwin, were forced underground in the 1790s by the repressive policies of Pitt's government, alarmed by events in France. This partly accounts for the obscurity of Blake's later writings and may have encouraged him to express a greater proportion of his most deep-felt beliefs in pictorial form. The end of all hopes for political reform and the distortion of the ideas of the French Revolution may also have helped to produce the feeling of despairing nihilism that marks Blake's works of the mid 1790s, a development epitomised in the difference between the *Songs of Innocence* of 1789 and the *Songs of Experience* that Blake added to them in 1794. However, from about 1800 he began to reconcile the presence of evil and material existence with a renewed faith in Christianity, though his Christianity was always anything but orthodox.

After a few tentative intimations in his early lyrical poems and the satirical *An Island in the Moon*, Blake's philosophy found written expression in a series of epic Prophetic Books. In these he evolved what can be called his own mythology. Personages such as Urizen, Los, Enitharmon and Orc struggle in a primaeval world of frozen depths, tormenting fires and globules of blood. They symbolise the successive subdivisions of the original, innocent man into the individual elements that made up his unified being. The most important are his reason, his imagination, his passions and his senses, which, once divided, war jealously against each other. Blake regarded this process of subdivision as the real Fall of Man, and the orthodox doctrine of Original Sin and the whole idea of a vengeful Jehovah were repugnant to him.

Blake's mythological figures, and the awesome

situations in which they find themselves, are most closely paralleled in Blake's illustrations to his own poems, but even his seemingly direct illustrations to the Bible, Shakespeare, Milton and Dante reflect his own philosophical ideas and their expression in his writings. This means that although Blake's best pictures are fully satisfying on their visual merits, one's appreciation can be immensely enriched by a knowledge of Blake's ideas.

Blake was born in 1757 and died in 1827. All but three years of his life were spent in London. At the age of ten he entered Henry Par's drawing school and in 1772 he was apprenticed to James Basire, the engraver. This apprenticeship was important both for the opportunity it gave Blake to see engravings by and after Old Masters, particularly Michelangelo, Raphael and Dürer, and for the time he spent in Westminster Abbey copying tombs for archaeological publications. It also established him as a professional engraver. In 1779 he entered the Royal Academy Schools, but he disliked the emphasis placed by his teachers on painterly qualities and drawing from life.

The power and originality of Blake's images has led to the idea that he was an untutored original. This was far from the case. He read widely, including the mystical writings of Emanuel Swedenborg, Jakob Boehme and the Neo-Platonists, and his pictorial style was firmly rooted in the style and tastes of his time, though it was to develop into a subtle and very personal creation.

'The Penance of Jane Shore' (plate 1) is a version of a work painted about 1779, one of a group of early historical watercolours which echo, albeit rather feebly, the history-pieces of Benjamin West, Gavin Hamilton and John Hamilton Mortimer (examples in the Tate Gallery are West's 'Cleombrotus ordered into Banishment by Leonidas II, King of Sparta', Hamilton's 'Priam pleading with Achilles for the Body of Hector', and Mortimer's 'Progress of Virtue' series). The elongated idealised figures with their sculptural draperies and poses are in the neo-classical style that was considered suitable for elevated classical and historical subjects. In addition the unscholarly historicism of 'Strawberry Hill' Gothic is reflected in the pseudomedieval trimmings of the costumes and weapons. The bearing of Edward IV's mistress Jane Shore at the ordeal imposed on her by Richard III had already been cited as an object of admiration by 18th-century historians; Blake probably chose the subject, and others like it, in protest against orthodox morality.

Blake's approach towards a more refined neo-classicism was strengthened by his friendship with John Flaxman, the sculptor. This can be seen in the much more accomplished 'Oberon, Titania and Puck with Fairies dancing' (plate 3), with the delightful swaying movement of its dancing figures. The subject may have been suggested by John Boydell's scheme for a Shakespeare Gallery of paintings by leading British artists, initiated in 1786. Blake's lowly position in the art-world of his time is shown by the fact that he was not even asked to contribute as an engraver.

A more forceful work is the drawing (plate 4) for the engraving of 'Job, his Wife and his Friends' of about the same date. In this there is more of the Grand Manner and a certain *terribilità* deriving from the large history-pieces of James Barry (such as the Tate Gallery's 'King Lear weeping over the dead Body of Cordelia') which were much admired by Blake.

Although Blake exhibited a few works at the Royal Academy and elsewhere from 1780 onwards, his pictures never gave him a living by themselves. The usual 18th-century expedient, first practised on a large scale by Hogarth, was to seek a wider market through engravings. Blake however was less successful with his engravings of his own works than with engravings after other artists, such as the book illustrations of his friend Thomas Stothard. These influenced such works as the simple and charming 'Age teaching Youth', with the boy's decoratively patterned costume. The delicate intimacy of this little watercolour of the later 1780s recalls Blake's early lyrics.

The greatest achievement of Blake's early years was in the field of poetry but in the 1790s the position began to alter. The changing relationship between the two branches of his art can be seen most readily in the development of his illuminated books. In these his own illustrations are welded to his texts with a singleness of inspiration perhaps unequalled in the history of art. At first, as in the early copies of *Songs of Innocence*, first issued in 1789, both text and illustrations were printed in relief and the illustrations were then coloured by hand in watercolour. Many of the designs were intertwined with the writing on the page in a manner reminiscent of medieval illuminations. In the books of the early 1790s such as *The Marriage of Heaven and Hell*, c. 1790–3, *Visions of the Daughters of Albion* and *America*, both of 1793, and *Europe*, 1794, the illustrations became more and more important in relation to the text, becoming rather more distinct from it at the same time. Finally, in *Urizen*, also of 1794, the designs, now completely separate as either whole-page or half-page illustrations, came to overwhelm the text

entirely. This was partly because of their sheer compositional weight and partly the result of a new technique whereby the colours were printed in thick pigments. This medium is a sort of tempera invented by Blake and was probably based on carpenter's glue rather than the traditional egg-yolk. It gives a much heavier, richer effect than the watercolour of the earlier books.

The illuminated books fall outside the scope of the Tate Gallery but can be studied in the Print Room of the British Museum. The Tate does however possess examples of the next stage in the evolution of the illustrations. By 1794–5 Blake felt he could issue some of them separately, in 'a selection from the different Books of such as could be Printed without the Writing, tho' to the Loss of some of the Best things. For they when Printed perfect accompany Poetical Personifications & Acts, without which Poems they never could have been Executed' (letter to Dawson Turner, 9 June 1818). The frontispiece from *Visions of the Daughters of Albion* (plate 2) is an outstanding example of Blake's colour-printing, a few final touches being added in pen and watercolour. *Visions of the Daughters of Albion* treats of the stultifying effects of orthodox sexual morality and also refers to recent political events. In the frontispiece the girl Oothoon, 'the soft soul of America', is fettered to Bromion who has ravished her; her former lover Theotormon, persuaded that she is now impure, crouches in despair. The cave-like setting and heavy clouds add to the oppressive gloom.

The separate publication of these small designs heralded the larger colour prints of 1795 (front cover and plates 6–11). With their bold images, clear-cut forms and rich texture the 1795 prints are arguably Blake's greatest works. Their technique is akin to that developed in the illuminated books. A similar form of tempera, sometimes referred to by Blake as 'fresco', was used, and the design was first painted in reverse on a sheet of millboard or similar material. A number of impressions, usually three, were then made on paper. The tacky paint produced a rich mottled surface and could be worked on further while still wet; an instance is the use of scratched lines to indicate rain in 'Pity' (plate 8). The effects obtainable can be seen at their most subtle in 'Newton' (plate 10), producing the effect of a rock covered with lichen and other foliage. Finally the prints were finished in pen and watercolour, the first impression requiring least attention whereas the subsequent ones, having received less of the tempera, needed more.

The prints also display Blake's richest effects of colour. 'Newton', 'Nebuchadnezzar' and 'Elohim creating Adam' (plates 10, 11 and front cover) are in blended tones of deep but glowing greens, blues and pinks. 'God judging Adam' (plate 7) and 'The Good and Evil Angels' are bolder, dominated by broad clearly defined areas of red and orange, while 'Pity' and 'Hecate' (plates 8 and 9) are in sombre, steely blues.

Their range of subject is bafflingly wide. Twelve titles are known, the Tate Gallery having examples of all but two, 'Satan exulting over Eve' and 'Naomi entreating Ruth and Orpah to return to the Land of Moab'. At first sight it is difficult to see the connection between subjects drawn from such diverse sources as the Old and New Testaments, Shakespeare and Milton; strangest of all is the presence of Newton, crouching in the nude with his compasses (plate 10). Yet there seems

to be no doubt that the group was conceived as a whole and that the clue to the prints' meaning, though not yet fully unravelled, lies in Blake's writings. Though no complete parallels can be found, each print seems to illustrate a stage in man's Fall, as described in particular in *Urizen*, 1794, and the unfinished manuscript *Vala* or *The Four Zoas*, on which Blake was working between about 1796 and 1807.

The first print of the series, the terrifying 'Elohim creating Adam' (front cover), shows Blake's rejection of the orthodox accounts of the Creation and Fall in the Old Testament. The title, inscribed below the design in Blake's hand, uses one of the Hebrew names of God and can be linked with the line added to *The Four Zoas* in about 1805, 'They sent Elohim, who created Adam to die for Satan'. Blake represents the Creation of the worm-entwined Adam as the first stage of the Fall; the creation of man in material form begins the fatal process of his division into separate warring entities. The placing of Elohim's two hands emphasises most expressively that the agonised Adam is being formed out of the matter of the earth, to which he is bound by the worm, symbol of mortality.

After this representation of man as brute matter 'Nebuchadnezzar' (plate 11), a close but imaginative rendering of the lines in *The Book of Daniel*, shows him at his most animal, a slave to the senses. 'Newton' (plate 10), which seems to have been composed as a pendant, shows him as slave to reason, unillumined by the imagination, a state particularly abhored by Blake. A similar figure had already appeared as a plate in *There is no Natural Religion*, *c.* 1788, accompanying the text, 'He who sees the Infinite in all things, sees God. He who sees the Ratio only, sees himself only'. There is also a connection, typical of the complex working of Blake's artistic processes, with the famous 'Ancient of Days', the frontispiece to *Europe*, 1794 (an example is in the British Museum), which shows God creating the universe with a pair of compasses, and through this with the frontispiece to the 1729 edition of Newton's *Principia*, on which the conception of 'The Ancient of Days' is based. The 'Newton' print itself is based on Michelangelo's Abias from the ceiling of the Sistine Chapel. Blake copied this figure from an engraving, never, unlike most of his contemporaries, having the opportunity to visit Italy and see the works of his idols in the original. A further aspect of the Fall seems to be illustrated in 'Lamech and his two Wives'. In this very obscure subject from *Genesis* the murderer Lamech, Cain's great-great-great-grandson, is shown ossified into a treelike form as if to stress his material nature.

The difficulty of interpreting these prints is shown in the case of 'God judging Adam' (plate 7), yet another condemnation of the orthodox Christian view of the Fall. This design was known for over a hundred years as 'Elijah in the fiery Chariot' but its real subject, recorded in 1805, has now been recognised: the stern Jehovah imposes his will on the stricken Adam, who is shown aged into the likeness of his condemner. There is a striking resemblance between the figure of God and the character Urizen, described and illustrated in Blake's illuminated books. An elderly, bearded man embodying the tyranny of pure reason, he was associated by Blake with the Jehovah of the Old Testament; it is he who creates the world in 'The Ancient of Days'. The print echoes a passage in the book *Urizen* of 1794, in which he declaims

his unyielding laws, whereupon 'All the seven deadly sins of the soul' appear 'in the flames of eternal fury'.

The same old man, even more forbidding in aspect, appears as Death in 'The House of Death' (plate 6). This can be interpreted as showing Jehovah, in the guise of Urizen, presiding over the ultimate decay of his material creation. The subject, from Milton's *Paradise Lost*, was also treated by Blake's friend Henry Fuseli, who shared his enthusiasm for Michelangelo, Shakespeare and Milton and pointed the way for Blake in the portrayal of what the late 18th century termed 'horrible imaginings'.

'Pity' (plate 8) strikes one at once with the inspired literalism with which it follows every image suggested by the lines in *Macbeth:*

And pity, like a naked new-born babe.
Striding the blast, or heaven's cherubin, hors'd
Upon the sightless couriers of the air. . . .

But it also alludes to another stage in man's fall. In *Urizen* the emotion of pity so disturbs the Eternal Prophet, Los, that 'the first female form' separates itself from his body and is called Pity or Enitharmon, once again subtracting from the completeness of the original man. That Blake, with his horror of social injustice, regarded pity as a negative virtue is shown by the opening lines of 'The Human Abstract' from *Songs of Experience*, 1794:

Pity would be no more,
If we did not make somebody Poor:
And Mercy no more would be,
If all where as happy as we.

The companion 'Hecate' (plate 9) represents

superstition, which also seems to have been regarded by Blake as a product of woman in the fallen world. The two designs not in the Tate Gallery, 'Satan exulting over Eve' and 'Naomi entreating Ruth and Orpah to return to the land of Moab,' seem to complete a quartet of subjects dealing with the place of women in Blake's overall scheme; there is an example of the latter in the Victoria and Albert Museum.

'The Good and Evil Angels' (Blake's own title) is the only one of the series not to have some basis in history or literature. It is a fascinating example of a development in purely visual terms of images from Blake's own writings. An earlier stage in the evolution of the design is the watercolour of 'Los and Orc' (plate 5), in its turn a variant of an illustration to *America*, 1793. This shows Los together with Enitharmon (who is omitted from the Tate Gallery's watercolour) standing in horror over their son Orc, who is bound to a rock by the chain of Los' jealousy. The incident is referred to in *America* and *Urizen* but not fully described until a passage in *Vala* or *The Four Zoas* of *c*. 1796–7. In the large colour print the chained figure of Orc, a character symbolising boundless energy, is shown fully grown and blind against a background of flame. Blake probably meant to show how, as the result of the fetters restraining it, Orc's energy has become perverted and sterile. A second figure, in appearance like Los in the watercolour, protects a terrified child from Orc's malevolence, but neither child nor incident can be found in Blake's writings and their precise significance is uncertain. Nevertheless the print is charged with expression and is fully convincing visually.

Much of the power of these prints derives from their purely destructive negation of conventional morality and accepted religion. The last of the group, 'Christ appearing to the Apostles after the Resurrection,' has been held to reflect Blake's continued faith in the God of the New Testament. On the other hand one is tempted to regard even this work as an attack on the superstitious belief in miracles or as a criticism of those who, like Doubting Thomas, need material evidence of a visionary event:' . . . because you Murder him he arises Again & you deny that he is Arisen & are blind to Spirit' (*The Everlasting Gospel*, c. 1818).

The amazing originality of these prints is unequalled in Blake's work. In no other works was he so free from the outside pressures created by his continued failure to find adequate recognition for his genius. By the end of the 1790s he had indeed secured a humble but constant patron in the government clerk Thomas Butts, who for many years paid a guinea each for a regular supply of Blake's works, but this must have exerted some influence on Blake's choice of subjects. Butts began in 1799 by commissioning fifty small pictures of subjects from the Bible. At least forty tempera paintings were finished in 1799 and 1800, and the series was continued with over eighty watercolours painted between 1800 and about 1805. The temperas were painted in much the same medium as the colour prints. Despite the visionary nature of his art, Blake believed that it should express his concepts with the greatest possible clarity and precision, and he hoped that his temperas would recapture the clear outlines and colours of the Renaissance. Unfortunately, except for some late examples, they have usually darkened and decayed.

This is particularly the case of the few painted on copper, such as 'The Agony in the Garden' (plate 13), now sadly disfigured by losses of paint. Nevertheless this remains one of his most expressive pictures with its dark glowing colours and the striking action of its two main figures. In its weight and dramatic power this painting recalls the large colour prints but others of the temperas are marked by a new grace and delicacy, for instance the sensuous 'David spying on Bathsheba at the Bath' (plate 12) and the hushed but poignant 'Procession from Calvary.'

The same variety of mood is found among the Biblical watercolours of *c*. 1800–5. The forcefulness of the 1795 colour prints is again present in 'The Blasphemer' (plate 16) with its Michelangelesque central figure and the expressive symmetry of his tormentors. On the other hand Blake's early neo-classical figures are recalled in a number of the watercolours, for instance 'The River of Life' (plate 15). The feeling of movement and the light gay colours of this subject from the *Apocalypse* are in contrast to the rigid poses and near monochrome of 'The Crucifixion: Behold Thy Mother' and 'The Entombment', so well attuned to their themes.

'The Four and Twenty Elders' (plate 18), another illustration to the *Apocalypse*, is listed in an account with Butts of 1805 and is presumably one of the last works in the series. The poses of the figures are more relaxed and the drawing and colouring softer, anticipating Blake's later style. The Tate Gallery also owns Blake's pencil sketch for this watercolour (plate 19). Although he sometimes appeared to claim that his pictures were direct copies of visions, this drawing shows that in fact he followed normal artistic practice in elaborating his finished works from rough sketches; many other cases are known.

'Satan in his original Glory' (plate 17) is outstanding in its jewel-like detail. Alas, the original blues have faded, reducing the colours to a rather subdued grey and orange. Here one can perhaps apply to Blake himself his saying about Milton—that he was 'of the Devil's party without knowing it' (*The Marriage of Heaven and Hell*, *c*. 1790–3) —except that Blake probably did know it. This is suggested by many of the epigrams in the same book, for example 'Without Contraries there is no progression. . . . From these contraries spring what the religious call Good & Evil. Good is the passive that obeys Reason. Evil is the active springing from energy'.

Most of the pictures of subjects from the Bible are more orthodox. In part this was necessitated by the nature of Butts' commission, but it also reflects a move away from Blake's previous outright rejection of accepted religion. This was part of a general change in his ideas, characterised by a more optimistic outlook and by a new acceptance of material, sensuous existence. The change seems to have occurred about the time he left London in 1800 to live for three years at Felpham, near Chichester, in a cottage found for him by another patron, the poet and biographer William Hayley. The tasks set him by Hayley—miniature portraits, engravings for his biographies, a decorative frieze of the heads of poets for his library— soon became uncongenial; nevertheless it was during these years that Blake seems to have begun to revise his manuscript of *Vala* or *The Four Zoas* in order to introduce specifically Christian ideas, while in *Milton*, which was begun in this period, he suggests that salvation can be achieved through the recognition and experience of error. It was also at Felpham that Blake painted one of his very rare landscapes, the visionary 'Landscape at Felpham' (plate 14), itself a mark of his reconciliation with nature.

Rather later than the Biblical watercolours is the highly finished 'Epitome of James Hervey's "Meditations among the Tombs"'. This is an allegorical summary of a typical 18th-century writing on mortality of the kind that still enjoyed a vogue at the turn of the century. Edward Young's *Night Thoughts* and Robert Blair's *The Grave*, for each of which Blake did a series of illustrations, are other examples. The 'Epitome', with its multitude of figures arranged on the surface in a dense, nearly symmetrical pattern, is close to a number of pictures of 'The Last Judgment' done in the years 1806–10 and like them was probably inspired by Michelangelo's fresco of that subject in the Sistine Chapel.

Blake's most uncompromising attempt to win recognition occurred in 1809, when he held an exhibition of his paintings at his brother's house in Soho. This laid particular stress on his temperas. He wrote his own *Descriptive Catalogue*, which contained long analyses of the pictures and an introduction in which he opposed the true method of colouring of Raphael, Michelangelo and Dürer to the false processes of Titian, Correggio and Rubens. The first two pictures in the catalogue were 'The Spiritual Form of Nelson guiding Leviathan' (plate 21) and 'The Spiritual Form of Pitt guiding Behemoth' (plate 20). Of these he wrote, 'Clearness and precision have been the chief objects in painting these Pictures. Clear colours unmudded by oil, and firm and determined lineaments unbroken by shadows, which ought to display and not hide form, as is the practice of the latter schools of Italy and Flanders'. Gold was used in the 'Pitt' in emulation of early Renaissance pictures.

Blake described these pictures as 'compositions of a mythological cast, similar to those Apotheoses of Persian, Hindoo, and Egyptian Antiquity, which are still preserved on rude monuments, being copies from some stupendous originals now lost or perhaps buried till some happier age. . . .The Artist wishes it was now the fashion to make such monuments, and then he should not doubt of having a national commission to execute these two Pictures on a scale that is suitable to the grandeur of the nation, who is the parent of his heroes, in high finished fresco, where the colours would be as pure and as permanent as precious stones, though the figures were one hundred feet in height'.

Like Newton in the series of colour prints, Nelson and Pitt were chosen as 'modern Heroes', in this case to express an Apocalyptic vision of war. The relationship to the Apocalypse is made clear by the continuation of the title of the 'Pitt': 'he is that Angel who, pleased to perform the Almighty's orders, rides on the whirlwind, directing the storms of war: He is ordering the Reaper to reap the Vine of the Earth, and the Plowman to plow up the Cities and Towers'.

'The Bard', the other tempera from Blake's exhibition now in the Tate, illustrates Gray's poem. This was a fairly common subject for painters at the time but was chosen by Blake to demonstrate the power of poetry over military might: Edward I, invading Wales, is smitten with terror by a solitary Bard who, accompanied by the spirits of his murdered colleagues, prophesies his doom and that of his line.

Among the other works in the exhibition were

the famous 'Canterbury Pilgrims' (now at Pollok House, near Glasgow) and an early drawing of 'above Thirty Years ago', included to show 'that the productions of our youth and of our maturer age are equal in all essential points'. This was either the Tate's 'Penance of Jane Shore' (plate 1) or the earlier smaller version.

The exhibition was a complete failure. Few people attended; no works were sold, except perhaps to Thomas Butts. For the next ten years Blake's life is practically unrecorded, though he continued to paint watercolours for Butts, mainly of subjects from Milton and *The Book of Job*, and produced *Jerusalem*, his longest and most richly illuminated book. He also undertook much more mundane tasks, such as engraving Wedgwood-ware for the firm's stock-books.

In 1818 his fortunes were radically altered by his meeting with John Linnell. This young portrait and landscape painter came to fill the place of Thomas Butts earlier in Blake's career, paying him regular sums of money in exchange for most of his output. He was also instrumental in introducing Blake to a number of young admirers, including the artists Samuel Palmer, Edward Calvert and George Richmond who were particularly attracted by a relatively minor offshoot of Blake's art, the exquisite woodcuts illustrating Dr. Thornton's edition of *The Pastorals of Virgil* published in 1821.

Earlier Linnell had introduced Blake to his teacher John Varley, an introduction that resulted in the most notorious works of Blake's career, the drawings known as 'Visionary Heads' (plates 24 and 25). Varley, a landscape painter in watercolours and an important teacher, also dabbled in astrology and physiognomy and was fascinated by Blake's visionary powers. In 1828 he published the first and only part of a projected four-volume *Treatise on Zodiacal Physiognomy*, with engravings by Linnell after some of Blake's drawings. These drawings date mainly from 1819 and 1820, when Blake would visit Varley in the evening and sketch his supposed visitants long into the night. He seems to have humoured the over-credulous Varley in the material presence of his 'sitters', most of whom were Biblical or historical personages such as Solomon, Socrates, Richard Coeur-de-Lion and Wat Tyler. Among the more outstanding of his inventions are the Tate Gallery's 'The Man who taught Blake painting in his Dreams' and 'The Man who built the Pyramids' (plate 24), fascinating examples of imaginative caricature.

Still more curious is Varley's account of the Tate's drawing of 'The Ghost of a Flea', which has recently been found to come from a rediscovered sketchbook first used by Varley and then in 1819 by Blake for many of his Visionary Heads. 'I felt convinced by his mode of proceeding that he had a real image before him, for he left off, and began on another part of the paper to make a separate drawing of the mouth of the Flea, which the spirit having opened, he was prevented from proceeding with the first sketch, till he had closed it. During the time occupied in completing the drawing, the Flea told him that all fleas were inhabited by the souls of such men as were by nature blood-thirsty to excess. . . . This spirit afterwards appeared to Blake, and offered him a view of his whole figure.' This second visit resulted in the Tate's extraordinary little painting in tempera heightened with gold (plate 25), a masterpiece of eccentricity only equalled in British art by some of the paintings of Richard Dadd.

This painting is still characterised by the heavy paint and dark tonality of most of Blake's earlier temperas. His last works in this medium have a new clarity of tone and sharpness of drawing, the result of being painted much more thinly over a white ground on panel, and have survived in nearly perfect condition. The two examples in the Tate Gallery, painted *c.* 1826, are both reworkings of earlier compositions. 'The Body of Abel found by Adam and Eve; Cain, who was to bury it, fleeing from the Face of his parents' (plate 22) is a more compact and powerful version of the watercolour included in Blake's exhibition in 1809. As well as the smoother, more finished handling there is a new delicacy of line and modelling, particularly apparent in the exquisite neck and arms of Eve.

The other tempera of *c.* 1826, 'Satan smiting Job with Sore Boils' (plate 23), is Blake's last statement of a composition developed in his two groups of watercolours illustrating *The Book of Job*, painted probably sometime about 1810 and in 1821–2 respectively, and in the subsequent engravings of 1823–5. Here again the design is tightened up, and the figure of Satan is made much more imposing and inhuman by the addition of large bat-like wings. As in the case of so many of Blake's illustrations to other authors, it has been established that the Job series embodies his own reinterpretation of the text. Whereas the Old Testament Job is a just man who becomes little more than a passive sufferer in the contest between God and Satan, Blake gave the story a more positive meaning by suggesting that Job's punishment was a consequence of his self-centred observance of 'The Letter that Killeth' of conventional religion. In this design Job is being tormented with the 'disease of shame' (*Jerusalem*) while his rejected wife crouches at his feet.

The engravings for *The Book of Job* were one of the two big schemes that, encouraged by Linnell, occupied Blake's last years. The other was his series of illustrations to Dante's *Divine Comedy* (plates 26–32). This series too was to be engraved but Blake died having completed only seven plates. He left, however, over a hundred large designs, some merely sketched in pencil, some completely finished in glowing watercolours, of which the Tate has twenty. Samuel Palmer gives an evocative description of the venerable visionary at work. 'On Saturday, 9th October, 1824, Mr. Linnell called and went with me to Mr. Blake. We found him lame in bed, of a scalded foot (or leg). There, not inactive, though sixty-seven years old, but hard-working on a bed covered with books sat he up like one of the Antique patriarchs, or a dying Michael Angelo. Thus and there was he making in the leaves of a great book (or folio) the sublimest designs from his (not superior) Dante. He said he began them with fear and trembling. I said: "O! I have enough of fear and trembling!" "Then", said he, "you'll do".'

These designs show Blake's mastery of watercolour in his late years, displaying a new sensuousness and variety of touch. This is most obvious in the jewel-like 'Beatrice addressing Dante from the Car' (plate 31). The sinuous figures show Blake's complete assimilation of the neo-classical idiom that still jars in some of his earlier works. The gracefulness and virtuosity of Blake's treatment of the figure is especially clear in the endlessly varied interplay between Dante and his companion Virgil; examples can be seen in 'Dante and Virgil penetrating the Forest' (plate 28), 'The Inscription over the Gate' (plate 27) and 'The Ascent of the Mountain of Purgatory.' The first also shows Blake's delight in the burgeoning forms of nature, a delight that had so strong an effect on the young Samuel Palmer.

There is a great variety of mood within the series. In contrast to the gentle narrative of the examples already mentioned are the forceful 'Cerberus', 'Plutus' and 'The Punishment of the Thieves'. 'The Simoniac Pope' (plate 26) is outstanding in its feeling of energy and movement, while 'Dante and Virgil approaching the Angel who guards the Entrance of Purgatory' (plate 30) has the oppressive quality of the colour prints of 1795.

Two of the drawings, one in America, the other in the British Museum, bear long inscriptions condemning Dante's conventional views on salvation. 'Every thing in Dante's Comedia shows That for Tyrannical Purposes he has made This World the Foundation of All & the Goddess Nature [i.e.] Memory is his Inspirer & not Imagination [i.e.] the Holy Ghost'. 'Whatever Book is for Vengeance for Sin & whatever Book is Against the Forgiveness of Sins is not of the Father but of Satan the Accuser & Father of Hell'. So the sun becomes more and more clouded over in the drawings showing Dante and Virgil ascending the Mountain of Purgatory, and the Angel guarding the entrance (plate 30) bears a strong likeness to Urizen, Blake's old symbol of the unimaginative imposition of orthodox religion. This condemnatory interpretation of the Angel is reinforced by the sombre colouring, the watercolour being dominated by greyish purples and blacks. Even the gaily coloured and at first sight joyous 'Beatrice addres-sing Dante from the Car' (plate 31) has been shown to be a criticism of Dante's view of the Terrestrial Paradise, where this scene takes place. For Dante, Beatrice symbolised the Church; Blake saw her also as the embodiment of the Female Will and equated her with his own character Rahab, the fallen state of Vala who symbolised Nature. Blake emphasised her dominance over Dante by giving her a crown, and the watercolour thus represents the subjection of the Poetic Genius, Dante, to the distorted doctrines of the Church in the fallen world.

Others of the designs also incorporate Blake's own commentary on Dante. The poets in 'Homer and the Ancient Poets' are shown in a sort of Druid thicket below a pagan altar and illustrate Blake's condemnation, on another of the drawings, of 'the Poetry of the Heathen, Stolen & Perverted from the Bible, not by Chance but by design, by the Kings of Persia & their Generals, the Greek Heroes & lastly by the Romans', and his exclamation, in On Homer's Poetry of c. 1820, 'The Classics, it is the Classics! & not Goths nor Monks, that Desolate Europe with Wars'. Similarly 'The Primaeval Giants sunk in the Soil' typify the five senses sunk in the bog of materialism. In other designs, such as 'The Simoniac Pope' (plate 26) and 'Plutus', Blake was content with direct illustration, agreeing with Dante on the sinfulness of simony and avarice, which have their basis in a materialistic view of life.

In the last but one of the existing illustrations, 'Dante in the Empyrean, drinking at the River of Life' (plate 32), Blake achieves a synthesis of his ideas with those of Dante, a synthesis that also sums up his own views of salvation. To the figure of Dante, the only one specified in the text, he adds three others together with a scene of artists at work. This last is on the left, above Dante and accompanies the figure of an aged poet, perhaps the regenerate Urizen, while on the right are two female figures, Enion and Vala, also in their regenerate state, who symbolise Nature. The river and the clump of foliage on the left are alive with tiny figures or 'infant joys'. The whole scene represents the regeneration of Art and Nature in the Eternal World as the result of the poet's drinking at the River of Life or Divine Imagination. The state of ultimate salvation, unlike the original state of innocence, accepts and transcends the full gamut of experience. In this vision Blake not only demonstrated the essential role of the artist in achieving salvation, but also summed up the pattern of his own life in arriving at this solution.

FOR FURTHER READING:

Alexander Gilchrist *Life of William Blake* 1863; 2nd edition 1880.

Mona Wilson *The Life of William Blake* 1927; 2nd edition 1948; 3rd edition edited by Geoffrey Keynes 1971.

Northrop Frye *Fearful Symmetry, a Study of William Blake* 1947.

Geoffrey Keynes *William Blake's Engravings* 1950.

Albert S. Roe *Blake's Illustrations to the Divine Comedy* 1953.

David V. Erdman *Blake, Prophet against Empire* 1954; 2nd edition 1969.

Geoffrey Keynes *The Complete Writings of William Blake* 1957 and subsequent editions.

Anthony Blunt *The Art of William Blake* 1959.

G. E. Bentley, Jr. *Blake Records* 1969.

Geoffrey Keynes *Drawings of William Blake* 1970.

Ruthven Todd *William Blake the Artist* 1971.

A detailed catalogue of the Tate Gallery's Blake collection, with an introduction by Anthony Blunt, is available in *William Blake, a Complete Catalogue of the Works in the Tate Gallery* by Martin Butlin, 2nd edition, published by the Tate Gallery 1971.

1 *The Penance of Jane Shore in St. Paul's Church. c.* 1793(?)
   (replica of a work of *c.* 1779)
   Pen and watercolour, 9⅝ × 11⅝ in. (5898)

2 *Frontispiece to 'Visions of the Daughters of Albion'. c.* 1795 Colour printed relief etching finished in watercolour, $6\frac{3}{4} \times 4\frac{3}{4}$ in. (3373)

3 *Oberon, Titania and Puck with Fairies dancing. c.* 1785
Pencil and watercolour, 18¾ × 26½ in. (2686)

4 *Job, his Wife and his Friends. c.* 1786
  Pen and wash, $11\frac{7}{8} \times 17\frac{3}{4}$ in. (5200 recto)

5 *Los and Orc. c.* 1792–3
Pen and watercolour, $8\frac{9}{16} \times 11\frac{5}{8}$ in. (T.547)

6 *The House of Death.* 1795
   Colour print, finished in pen and watercolour, $19\frac{1}{8} \times 24$ in. (5060)

7 *God judging Adam.* 1795
  Colour print, finished in pen and watercolour, $17 \times 21\frac{1}{8}$ in. (5063)

8 *Pity. c.* 1795
Colour print, finished in pen and watercolour, $16\frac{3}{4} \times 21\frac{1}{4}$ in. (5062)

9 *Hecate. c.* 1795
   Colour print, finished in pen and watercolour, $17\frac{1}{4} \times 22\frac{7}{8}$ in. (5056)

10 *Newton.* 1795
   Colour print, finished in pen and watercolour, $18\frac{1}{8} \times 25\frac{5}{8}$ in. (5058)

11 *Nebuchadnezzar.* 1795
Colour print, finished in pen and watercolour, $17\frac{5}{8} \times 24\frac{3}{8}$ in. (5059)

12 *David spying on Bathsheba at the Bath. c.* 1799–1800
Tempera on canvas, 10⅜ × 14 13/16 in. (3007)

13 *The Agony in the Garden. c.* 1799–1800
Tempera on copper, $10\frac{5}{8} \times 15$ in. (5894)

14 *Landscape near Felpham.* 1800–3
Pencil and watercolour, $9\frac{3}{8} \times 13\frac{1}{2}$ in. (3964 xii)

15 *The River of Life. c.* 1805
  Pen and watercolour, 12 × 13¼ in. (5887)

16 *The Blasphemer*.
c. 1800
Pen and watercolour,
15 × 13⅜ in. (5195)

Satan in his Original Glory.
c. 1800–5
Pen and watercolour,
16⅞ × 13⅜ in. (5892)

18 *The Four and Twenty Eld*
c. 1805
Pencil and watercolour,
13 $\frac{15}{16}$ × 11 $\frac{1}{2}$ in. (5897)

*Sketch for The Four and Twenty Elders. c. 1805
Pencil, 19 × 15⅛ in.
(3694 i recto)*

20 *The Spiritual Form of Pitt guiding Behemoth.* 1805
Tempera on canvas,
$29\frac{1}{8} \times 24\frac{3}{4}$ in. (1110)

*The Spiritual Form of Nelson
guiding Leviathan. c.* 1805–9
Tempera on canvas,
30 × 24⅝ in. (3006)

22 *The Body of Abel found by Adam and Eve. c.* 1826
Tempera on panel, 12¾ × 17 in. (5888)

23 *Satan smiting Job with Sore Boils. c.* 1826
Tempera on panel, $12\frac{7}{8} \times 17$ in. (3340)

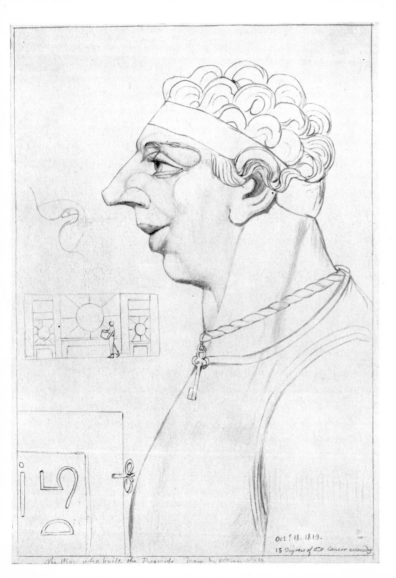

Oct.ʳ 18. 1819.

15 Degrees of ♋ Cancer ascending

The Man who built the Pyramids. Drawn by William Blake

24 *The Man who built the*
Pyramids. (? copy by John
Linnell). 1819 ?
Pencil, $11\frac{7}{8} \times 8\frac{1}{2}$ in. (5185

The Ghost of a Flea
1819
Tempera on panel,
$\frac{7}{16} \times 6\frac{3}{8}$ in. (5889)

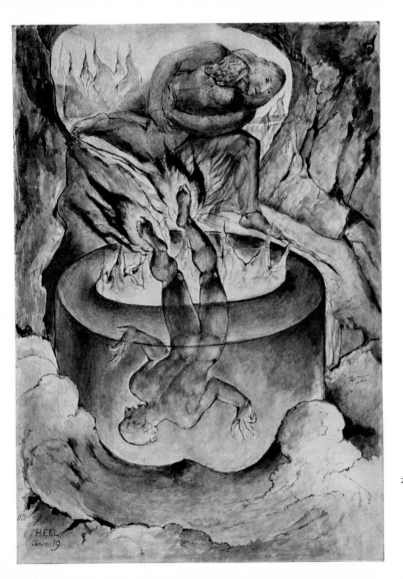

26 *The Simoniac Pope.* 1824
Pen and watercolour,
$20\frac{3}{4} \times 14\frac{1}{2}$ in. (3357)

The Inscription over the
Gate of Hell. 1824–7
Pen and watercolour,
10⅝ × 14½ in. (3352)

28 *Dante and Virgil penetrating the Forest.* 1824–7
Pencil, pen and watercolour, $14\frac{1}{2} \times 20\frac{5}{8}$ in. (3351)

29 *The Pit of Disease: the Falsifiers.* 1824–7
Pen and watercolour, 14⅝ × 20⅝ in. (3362)

30 *Dante and Virgil approach*
the Angel who guards the
Entrance of Purgatory. 18
Pencil, pen and watercolc
$20\frac{5}{8} \times 14\frac{5}{8}$ in. (3367)

31 *Beatrice addressing Dante from the Car.* 1824–7
Pen and watercolour, 14⅝ × 20¾ in. (3369)

32 *Dante in the Empyrean,*
drinking at the River of Li
1824–7
Pencil and watercolour,
$20\frac{5}{8} \times 14\frac{5}{8}$ in. (3370)